**DO NOT REMOVE
CARDS FROM POCKET**

VIETNAM
the land

Bobbie Kalman

The Lands, Peoples, and Cultures Series

Crabtree Publishing Company

The Lands, Peoples, and Cultures Series

Created by Bobbie Kalman

For Lori and Steve,
who look forward to discovering Vietnam

Editor-in-Chief
Bobbie Kalman

Writing team
Bobbie Kalman
Greg Nickles
Virginia Mainprize
Niki Walker

Text and photo research
David Schimpky

Managing editor
Lynda Hale

Editors
Greg Nickles
Virginia Mainprize
Niki Walker
Janine Schaub

Consultant
Nancy Tingley, Wattis Curator of
Southeast Asian Art, Asian Art
Museum of San Francisco

Computer design
Lynda Hale
Greg Nickles

Illustrations
Sarah Palleck: pages 4, 6
Barb Bedell: back cover

Special thanks to
Marc Crabtree, who, during a recent assignment in Vietnam, took
photographs that gave an accurate portrayal of modern Vietnam;
Lance Woodruff; Pierre Vachon and the Canadian International
Development Agency; the Vietnam Canada Trade Council; the World
Society for the Protection of Animals

Photographs
Jeffrey Alford/Asia Access: title page, pages 4-5 (bottom), 7 (bottom),
   20, 23 (bottom), 25 (top), 26 (bottom), 30
Jeanette Andrews-Bertheau: pages 9 (bottom), 21 (bottom), 22-23 (top)
Archive Photos: pages 14, 15 (top)
CIDA Photo/Cindy Andrew: pages 13, 15 (bottom), 25 (bottom)
Marc Crabtree: pages 5 (top), 7 (top), 10 (bottom left & right), 12,
   21 (top), 22 (bottom), 24 (top), 26 (top), 29 (both)
Wolfgang Kaehler: cover, pages 8 (both), 16-17 (both), 18, 19,
   24 (bottom), 27
Michael McDonell: pages 9 (top), 10-11 (top)
Larry Tackett/Tom Stack & Associates: page 28

Separations and film
Dot 'n Line Image Inc.

Printer
Worzalla Publishing Company

The Hoa Binh rice fields in northern Vietnam are shown on the cover.
The title page shows hills surrounding Mt. Fan Si Pan, also in
northern Vietnam. The bird on the back cover is a sarus crane, which
symbolizes loyalty and long life.

Published by
Crabtree Publishing Company

350 Fifth Avenue	360 York Road, RR 4,	73 Lime Walk
Suite 3308	Niagara-on-the-Lake,	Headington
New York	Ontario, Canada	Oxford OX3 7AD
N.Y. 10118	L0S 1J0	United Kingdom

Cataloging in Publication Data
Kalman, Bobbie, 1947-
   Vietnam: the land

(Lands, peoples, and cultures series)
Includes index.
ISBN 0-86505-223-9 (library bound) ISBN 0-86505-303-0 (pbk.)
This book examines the history, geography, agriculture, businesses,
transportation systems, and wildlife of Vietnam.

1. Vietnam - Description and travel - Juvenile literature. I. Title.
II. Series.

DS556.3.K35 1996   j959.7   LC 95-51992
                                                CIP

Contents

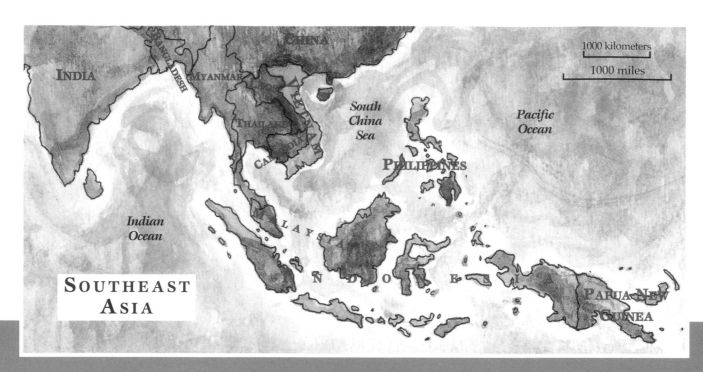

SOUTHEAST ASIA

A diverse land

With its magnificent mountains, lush rainforests, fertile farmlands, and spectacular beaches, Vietnam is a land of natural beauty. When many people think of Vietnam, however, they remember a country that was destroyed by a terrible war in the 1960s and 70s. This war was only a short part of Vietnam's long, eventful history.

Today, Vietnam is trying to overcome the damage and loss caused by the war and hopes to build a bright future. Rebuilding is difficult, especially for a country that has experienced so many problems. Recently, the government introduced new ideas to help the economy develop. Businesses and trade are already growing, cities are booming, and farmland is being used to produce more and better crops.

Facts at a glance:
Official name: Socialist Republic of Vietnam
Capital city: Hanoi
Population: 73,104,000 (1994)
Area: 325,560 square kilometers
      (125,708 square miles)
Official language: Vietnamese
Main religion: Buddhism
Currency: New dong
National holiday: Independence Day
      (September 2)

(top, inset) The red background in Vietnam's flag shows that the country has a communist government. The star stands for Vietnam's freedom.
(opposite page, inset) Vietnam is the yellow country on this map. From north to south it is nearly 1600 kilometers (1000 miles) long.
(left) Cam Ranh Bay, on Vietnam's central coast, was used by the Americans as a military base. Today, thousands of boats depart from this coast for the rich fishing grounds of the South China Sea.

On the map, labels include:

Dien Bien Phu
CHINA
Red River
HOANG LIEN MOUNTAINS
Hanoi • Haiphong
Ha Long Bay
Red River Delta
Gulf of Tonkin
LAOS
Mekong River
TRUONG SON MOUNTAINS
South China Sea
THAILAND
Hué
Da Nang
CAMBODIA
VIETNAM
Nha Trang
Cam Ranh
Gulf of Thailand
Ho Chi Minh City
Mekong River Delta

300 kilometers
300 miles

North to south

Vietnam is a long, narrow country stretching along the east coast of the Indochinese Peninsula in Southeast Asia. The Vietnamese say their country is shaped like a bent bamboo pole carrying a rice basket at each end. If you look at the map, you will see that Vietnam has an S shape—wide at the top and bottom and very narrow at the center. The country is divided into three geographic regions—the north, center, and south.

Mountains and hills

Most of Vietnam is covered by mountains and hills, which are called the highlands. The Truong Son mountain range runs from the north into the south and separates Vietnam from Laos and Cambodia, its neighbors to the west.

The Hoang Lien range rises in the north, crossing from northern Vietnam into southern China. These mountains are higher and rockier than those of the Truong Son and include Vietnam's highest peak, Fan Si Pan.

Thick forests of valuable hardwood trees cover half the highlands, and wild animals, such as tigers and elephants, roam through the remote jungles. A quarter of the population of Vietnam lives in villages throughout the highlands.

So much water!

More than two hundred rivers flow down from the mountains to Vietnam's long sea coast. Much of the land in between, known as the lowlands, is crisscrossed by rivers. The two longest, the Red River in the north and the Mekong River in the south, have formed wide **deltas**. Most people live in these lowland areas, either on farms or in large, busy cities.

Laos, Thailand, and Cambodia are Vietnam's neighbors to the west. China is to the northeast. These countries have influenced Vietnam's history and culture.

River deltas

The place where a river begins is called its **source**. As a river flows from its source, it picks up particles of soil and sand. The fast-moving water carries these particles along. When the river reaches its **mouth** at the sea, the current slows suddenly. The soil and sand sink and begin to pile up.

Over hundreds of years, the pile grows and blocks the mouth of the river. The river splits into two branches and flows around the pile. Over time, each branch becomes clogged, and the water must find new paths. Eventually, a network of streams and channels forms around the river's mouth. This network is called a **river delta**. Delta soil, known as silt, is very good for farming. It is rich in the nutrients that plants need. This wet, marshy land is also home to a wide variety of birds, reptiles, mammals, and aquatic life.

The northern highlands

The northern region, called Bac Bo, has two very different landscapes—the rugged highlands and the flat lowlands. In the highlands, some areas are still covered by dense jungle forests, but in others, the trees have been cut down for lumber or to clear land for farms. This area, rich in coal, tin, zinc, and lead, is also mined for its valuable minerals. Farmers and their families live in small villages scattered throughout the mountains and hills. They grow crops by building **terraces** on the rough hillsides.

The Red River and its delta

The Red River flows from China, down through the northern highlands on its way to the sea. Its water, reddish in color because of the silt it carries, has given the river its name. The wet, flat lowland area in Bac Bo is the Red River Delta, home to millions of Vietnamese. Hanoi, the country's capital, and Haiphong, a major seaport, are in this delta.

In the lowlands, the Red River floods its banks each year during the rainy season. Throughout the delta, canals have been dug, and walls of earth, called **dikes** and **levees**, have been built to help control the water flow. Even with these precautions, homes are often damaged, and sometimes people and animals drown. The floods, which dump silt onto the fields, are very important to millions of farmers. In this rich, wet earth they grow rice, Vietnam's most important crop and source of food.

Three thousand islands rise from Ha Long Bay, off the northern coast. These steep limestone rocks are actually the peaks of underwater mountains. Some people believe they are the homes of spirits.

Terraced farmlands

Farmers in the northern and central highlands use terraces to grow crops on steep hills. Terraces look like giant steps. When heavy rains fall on hills, fertile soil is washed down into valleys and streams. This process is called **soil erosion**. Terraces stop soil erosion because they are flat. The rainwater is held on the steps and soaks into the ground. In some countries, farmers have grown crops on terraces for thousands of years. Today, terraces are used in more places than ever before for growing a variety of crops. Modern farms use bulldozers and other machines to build terraces. In Vietnam, the terraces have been cut into the hills by hand!

The Central Highlands

The central region, called Trung Bo, is the narrowest part of Vietnam. The Truong Son Mountains form the hilly Central Highlands, where tea plants and rubber trees are grown.

Hill tribes, named *Montagnards* (which means "highlanders") by the French, live in the Central Highlands. Although there are several tribes, the population in this area is sparse. Farming is poorer here than in the fertile lowland deltas.

The coast

Most people in Trung Bo live along the long, narrow coast. They live in seaports, fishing villages, and on farms. Each day, thousands of boats head out to gather their catch of fish, a favorite food of many Vietnamese. Tourists enjoy visiting the scenic beaches along the South China Sea. This coast is beginning to change as new restaurants, hotels, and holiday resorts are being built.

(top) This beautiful beach along the central coast near Nha Trang is an excellent spot for water sports such as fishing, snorkeling, and scuba diving.
(circle) The highlands rise behind this farmer and his team of water buffalo. A thin strip of fields is farmed along Vietnam's central coast. The farmers work hard to grow their crops with only animals to help them.

Southern lowlands

Nam Bo is Vietnam's southern region. It is a huge, wet lowland area that contains the Mekong River Delta and several smaller deltas. Ho Chi Minh City, which is Vietnam's largest city, is near the Mekong Delta. Millions of people live there. Millions more live nearby in the fertile farmlands of the delta, which is one of the richest farming regions in the world. Canals cross this low, wet area, carrying water to the rice crops and transporting people and their goods.

Nine Dragons

The Vietnamese call the Mekong River "Nine Dragons" because it once had nine branches which flowed through Vietnam. The Mekong River is almost 4200 kilometers (2600 miles) long. Starting in the mountains of Tibet, it runs through China, Laos, and Cambodia before branching several times at the Mekong Delta. It empties into the South China Sea.

(circle) This farmer is carrying a load of rice through a lowland field. She uses a **don ganh,** *which is two baskets attached to a bamboo pole.*

(bottom) There are many rivers and canals in the southern lowlands. Thousands of families make their homes on boats that they also use for fishing and transportation.

9

Different climates

Vietnam is a tropical country. Tropical areas lie between the Tropic of Cancer and the Tropic of Capricorn, two horizontal lines near the equator. Tropical countries have warm weather most of the year.

Hot and cold

Vietnam is such a long country that the weather in the north and south can be quite different. Someone in the north might wake up to a cool morning, while someone in the south finds the day humid and hot. Altitude also influences climate. Weather in the highlands is cooler than in the lowlands.

The monsoon

Vietnam's weather is affected by winds called **monsoons**. From October to March, the monsoons blow from the northeast, overland from China, bringing dry weather with them. From May to September, the monsoons come from the opposite direction, sweeping up from the southwest. They blow across the ocean, picking up water and forming heavy rain clouds. When these monsoons hit land, the clouds dump torrential rains, which can cause severe flooding.

Dikes and levees usually control the floods, but sometimes the water rushes over them and causes terrible damage. Some houses near the water are built on stilts so the flood waters can flow harmlessly underneath. Despite the damage monsoon rains can cause, farmers depend on the rains and floods to bring water to their crops and fertile soil to their farmland.

Typhoon!

During the summer, violent tropical storms form over the Pacific Ocean and batter the coast. These **typhoons** bring thunderstorms, crashing waves, high winds, and heavy rains. Weather forecasters are able to give warnings when these storms are approaching, but people can do very little to prevent the damage they cause.

(above) During the summer monsoon, heavy rains fall on Vietnam, often causing floods. The rains help crops grow, and the floods bring nutrients to the soil. Unfortunately, the monsoon rains also bring destruction to homes and other buildings. Sometimes animals and people die.
(opposite page, left) Winters in the north can be chilly. This young boy has put on a wool hat to keep his head warm.
(opposite page, right) Umbrellas are a common sight on the beaches of Vietnam.

11

This temple was once part of Champa, a powerful kingdom in the south during the time the Chinese controlled the northern part of Vietnam.

Vietnam's past

The ancient kingdom of the Viet people was called Nam Viet. It was founded in the north around the Red River Delta.

Chinese rule

The Chinese invaded Nam Viet in 111 BC, not long after its formation. For over 1000 years, the Chinese controlled the region. The Viet people fought back many times, but the Chinese army was too strong. Although the Viet people did not like their Chinese rulers, they learned much from them about writing, farming, science, and government. While the Chinese ruled the north, two separate kingdoms, Champa and the Khmer empire, grew in the south.

In AD 938, the Viets defeated the Chinese army. For most of the next 900 years, the country was independent, ruled by its own emperors. Gradually, the Viets took over the southern lands. In 1802, the whole area was renamed Vietnam.

The colonial years

In the 1500s, Europeans sailed to Southeast Asia to buy products such as rice, silk, tea, and spices. The French were interested in more than trade. They knew that Vietnam had rich, fertile farmland, natural resources, and mineral deposits. France sent soldiers to take over Vietnam and, by the late 1800s, had divided it into three colonies.

French rule

The French developed large rubber and tea plantations, built factories, and dug mines. They forced the Vietnamese to work for very little money. They built churches and tried to change the religion of the Vietnamese. The Vietnamese had to pay high taxes and were not allowed to hold any important positions in government or business. Farmers revolted against their cruel landlords, and workers organized strikes, but the French stayed in control until World War II.

Some Vietnamese still can remember the time when French governors ruled the land. The French built many churches and converted people to Christianity.

Japanese control

During World War II, Japan took control of Vietnam for five years. After the war and the Japanese surrender in 1945, the Vietnamese hoped to form an independent country with their own leaders. France, however, wanted its colonies back. Soldiers were sent and, within a few months, France again controlled Vietnam.

The Vietnamese were determined to end French rule. They began to fight the French troops and finally forced them to surrender after the battle at Dien Bien Phu. When the French left Vietnam in 1954, the country was divided in two. The north was controlled by a **communist** government. The south was led by a corrupt government, supported by France and the United States. Elections were to be held in two years to reunite the country, but no elections took place. To protest, the Viet Cong, a group of South Vietnamese that supported the government of the north, began attacking villages in the south.

The Americans supported the government of South Vietnam because it was not communist. They were afraid that North Vietnam and its Viet Cong supporters would invade the south and place it under communist rule. In a communist country, the government owns and controls all the farms, industries, businesses, and banks. In 1964, the Americans began sending in hundreds of thousands of soldiers to help South Vietnam fight the Viet Cong. They called this fight the Vietnam War.

A bloody fight

Americans fought in this terrible, bloody war for nine years. Soldiers fought in fields, swamps, jungles, and villages. The Viet Cong killed anyone they thought was helping the Americans; the Americans killed people they thought were on the side of the Viet Cong.

Thousands of bombs were dropped on the north and south. About two million Vietnamese were killed, four million were wounded, and six million lost their homes. By 1973, when the Americans decided to leave, 58,000 of their soldiers were dead or missing. The fighting between the north and south continued for two more years. Finally, the North Vietnamese took over the south and united the country under a communist government.

Running from the war

The people of Vietnam suffered greatly during the war. Their villages were burned, cities were bombed, farms were destroyed, and innocent people were killed. Many became **refugees**, fleeing from their farms into the cities when the fighting came too close or there was no food. Thousands were forced to live in dirty refugee camps outside the cities because they had no homes, jobs, or money. After the war, a million people left Vietnam, hoping to find a safer home in another country. Thousands died at sea while trying to escape in overcrowded boats.

Agent Orange

During the war, the Viet Cong often hid in the thick jungles of South Vietnam. American planes dropped a chemical called **Agent Orange** onto the jungles to kill the trees and uncover the hideouts of the enemy soldiers. Agent Orange was very destructive—it killed about one-fifth of Vietnam's trees. The water and soil were poisoned, and crops were destroyed. Many people starved to death. People and animals were sometimes sprayed by passing planes. Since the war, the chemical has been blamed for causing disease and birth defects.

Painful memories

In recent years, the Vietnamese have been busily repairing the damage to their country. Despite their work, recovery has been slow. Ruins of buildings sit deserted, and roads, bridges, railroads, and factories need to be rebuilt. Most people have lost friends and family members who were killed or fled the country. Many who survived the wars were badly injured. In spite of so many setbacks, the people of Vietnam are working hard to turn their country into a growing and prosperous nation.

Soldiers in South Vietnam took villagers prisoner if they believed the farmers were helping the Viet Cong.

(top) Over eight million Americans served in Vietnam during nine years of the war.
(bottom) This vast graveyard is just one reminder of the millions of Vietnamese who were killed.

Vietnam's cities

Although most Vietnamese live on farms, many have settled in large cities and towns located in the lowlands or on the coast. Hanoi and Ho Chi Minh City are huge, crowded centers, whereas other cities, such as Hué and Da Nang, are smaller and quieter.

Hanoi

Hanoi was Vietnam's capital for 800 years until 1802. In 1945 it again became the capital and is now the center of government for a united Vietnam. Built on the banks of the Red River, its name means "city at the bend of the river." With a population of three million, it is Vietnam's second-largest city and an important industrial center in the north.

Hanoi's business section, hotels, and shops are in an area that was built by the French in colonial times. The wide streets are lined with trees, and the buildings have iron balconies and painted shutters. The city is famous for its many lakes and beautiful parks. In the heart of its downtown area is Hoan Kiem Lake, the Lake of the Restored Sword. It is surrounded by a large park where families and friends have picnics, fly kites, celebrate festivals, or just go for a stroll.

Hanoi's long history can be seen in its ancient temples and pagodas, built during Chinese rule. Some are almost 1000 years old. Vietnam's first university was built in Hanoi in 1076.

Ho Chi Minh City

Ho Chi Minh City and its surrounding farmland are home to four million people and cover a huge area of 2029 square kilometers (783 square miles) in the Mekong Delta. It has more businesses and industry than any other city in Vietnam. The streets are filled with bicycles, motorcycles, and a few cars and buses, and the sidewalks are crowded with people selling goods. There are many hotels and restaurants for the tourists and business people who visit the city.

Like Hanoi, the city has a French look, and many of the wide streets in the downtown area are lined with trees. Until 1976, this city was called Saigon. When it was taken over by the North Vietnamese army, it was renamed Ho Chi Minh City, after the leader who led the rebellion against French control.

Hué

Hué is a quiet city in central Vietnam with a population of 260,000 people. It is Vietnam's third-largest city and is an important cultural, educational, and religious center.

Hué was the capital and home of thirteen emperors from 1802 to 1945. A walled fort, called the Citadel, surrounds much of the city. Inside is the Forbidden Purple City where the emperors lived. Most of the Forbidden Purple City was destroyed during the Vietnam War. Many people are working to restore its beauty.

(left) Billboards advertising foreign companies tower over the busy streets of Ho Chi Minh City. This city has become a center of international business in Vietnam. (right) This archway in Hué is the gate to Emperor Tu Duc's tomb. Tu Duc reigned from 1848 to 1883.

17

Farming in Vietnam

Farming has been an important part of life in Vietnam for centuries. Even today, most people are farmers, working on small plots or on large government-run plantations.

Hard work

Farming in Vietnam is difficult, exhausting work because most farmers do not have tractors or other modern equipment. They use water buffalo to help with heavy work such as plowing or carrying loads. Other jobs, such as planting and harvesting, must be done by hand.

Rice—a vital crop

Rice has been farmed in Vietnam for thousands of years. Today, three-quarters of the country's farmland is used for growing this crop. Most rice farms are located in the river deltas. Because the deltas have rich soil, warm weather, and lots of water, farmers can grow two or three crops each year. Farmers now grow more rice than the Vietnamese need, so the extra rice is **exported**, or sold to other countries. Vietnam is the world's third-largest exporter of rice.

Other crops

Cash crops, which are farmed mainly to sell to other countries, are grown on large plantations. In the mist-covered hills of the highland regions, tea and coffee are harvested. In the south, rubber trees are tapped for their valuable sap, used in making rubber. Sugar cane, pepper, and peanuts are other valuable cash crops.

Many fruits and vegetables grow in Vietnam's moist, warm climate. Bananas, pineapples, mangoes, and coconuts are sold in the local markets. Sweet potatoes, tomatoes, snow peas, cabbage, and **cassava**, a shrub whose roots are eaten, are popular vegetable crops.

Vietnamese farmers grow a wide variety of crops, which are sold at town and city markets.

◈ Growing rice ◈

Rice is grown in fields called **paddies**. Some farmers grow it in either dry or flooded paddies. Others use a combination of dry and wet paddies. They scatter seeds in the dry paddy, water them, and wait for them to sprout into tiny plants, or **seedlings**, before moving them to a wet paddy.

Preparing the fields

It takes about one month for the seedlings to grow. During this time, the farmers busily prepare their wet fields for the little plants. They build low dikes around the paddies. All day long, entire families collect water in straw baskets and carry it back to flood the paddy. When the seedlings are tall enough, they are carefully pulled from the dry paddy, tied into bundles, and carried to the

flooded paddy. One by one, the seedlings are planted in neat rows in the mud. Even while the plants are growing, the farmers cannot rest. They are busy weeding and flooding their fields. As the plants grow, the water level in the paddy is raised. Soon the small rice plants grow tall and green, and all the hard work is rewarded.

Harvest time

When the rice plants turn gold, they are ready to be harvested. Farmers open the dikes to drain the water from the paddies. The rice plants are cut by hand, using a sharp, curved knife. They are then bundled and laid out in the sun to dry.

Farmers till their paddies to prepare for planting.

Threshing

Threshing, which separates the rice grains from the stalk of the plant, is usually done by beating the plants against bamboo poles. Farmers who live near a highway often spread their rice right onto the road. The hot, flat surface not only dries the grains faster, but passing cars and trucks drive over the rice and help with the threshing.

Milling and winnowing

When the rice is dry, it is gathered into large baskets and pounded. This **milling** process separates the rice kernel from its brown husk. In the final step, called **winnowing**, basketfuls of milled rice are tossed into the air so the wind can blow the light husks away from the kernels.

Nothing is wasted

Farmers use every part of the rice plant. The husks are fed to farm animals, and the stalks are woven into mats or used as fertilizer. After the family has taken what it needs for food, the rice kernels are gathered into sacks, ready to be shipped off to city markets or sold to other countries.

(top) Farmers in the delta regions grow rice in wet paddies, but farmers in the northern regions grow a different variety of rice using only dry paddies. (bottom) Farmers often dry rice on the side of a road. Passing cars and trucks drive over the rice and help with the threshing. A fan helps with winnowing.

Food from the sea

Each morning, the coastal villages of Vietnam come alive with activity as fishing boats prepare to set out to sea. Some boats are small and use oars, but most are sailboats or motorboats. At the end of the day, fish such as anchovies, mackerel, and snapper are hauled out of the sea in large nets. Men and women wait on the beach to help pull in the heavy catch. Prawns, crabs, and shrimp are caught in the inland waterways.

Fish farming

Farming fish is a popular business in Vietnam. To prevent them from escaping, the fish are kept in **pens**, which are enclosed parts of a river or stream. Farmers feed their fish special food to make them big and fat. Carp, catfish, and long river-dwelling fish called snakehead are among the fish raised in these farms. Shrimp are farmed in the canals of the Mekong River Delta.

Food and profit

Seafood is an important part of the Vietnamese diet. Millions of people depend on the catch for their daily meals. A salty fish sauce made from anchovies is a common cooking ingredient. Mixed with garlic, vinegar, and sugar, this sauce becomes *nuoc cham*, a tasty dip for many foods.

Many people also rely on fishing for their income. Fish caught off the coast are sold to other countries, especially Japan. Some Vietnamese sell their catch at fish markets, where people buy fresh seafood for their families or for restaurant customers.

(top) When fishing boats come into harbor, the catch is pulled ashore in large baskets. Carrying these heavy loads takes teamwork!
(right) Mieu Island is one of the most important fish-farming areas in Vietnam. The cuttlefish held by this farmer is not actually a fish; it is a close relative of the octopus and squid.
(opposite page, bottom) Fishing is often a family business in Vietnam. At a very young age, children begin learning fishing skills from their parents.

Transportation

Traveling long distances in Vietnam is difficult. Few people can afford cars, and many roads and bridges that were heavily bombed during the Vietnam War still need to be repaired. Trains are slow, and flying is expensive.

On the water

There are so many rivers and canals that one of the easiest ways to travel is on the water. Every day, thousands of boats transport people and goods from place to place. Small flat-bottomed boats, called **sampans**, travel rivers and streams. Long, narrow boats carry larger loads. Traditional sailboats, called **junks,** cruise along the coast.

Two wheels or three?

City streets are crowded with thousands of bicycles and motor scooters. The traditional Vietnamese taxi is the **lambretta**, a small three-wheeled vehicle. Another easy way of getting around the city is by *xich-lo*, or **cyclo**, a three-wheeled bicycle. It has a passenger seat in the front and one for the driver in the back.

Animal power

On the rough dirt roads of villages, animals are still an important means of transportation. Most farmers cannot afford a car or truck. Instead, they use water buffalo to pull carts.

The Reunification Express

When Vietnam was a colony, its French rulers built a railroad to connect Hanoi and Saigon. During the Vietnam War, the rail lines were damaged by bombing. After the country was united, the Vietnamese government began rebuilding the railroad to link the north and the south. Many sections of the track still need to be modernized. It takes three days for the slow-moving Reunification Express to make the journey between Hanoi and Ho Chi Minh City.

(opposite page, top) Round boats called **thung chai** *are used in the ocean near the town of Nha Trang. They are made of woven bamboo strips covered with tar.*
(opposite page, bottom) Bicycles of all kinds are an inexpensive means of travel for Vietnamese families.
(above) Highway One is an important roadway that connects the north and south.
(right) Buffalo boys are young workers who look after water buffalo.

New business

In 1975, after years of terrible warfare, the new nation of Vietnam faced the difficult task of rebuilding its **economy**. A country's economy is the organization and management of its businesses, industry, and money. In Vietnam, the communist government took control of the land, banks, and factories.

Rebuilding Vietnam

The fighting during the Vietnam War, and the damage it caused, made it difficult to do daily business. After the war, when the communist government took over the south, many business people fled, and Vietnam became very poor. After Vietnamese soldiers invaded Cambodia in 1978, many countries refused to trade raw materials or manufactured goods with Vietnam.

The government began building factories and setting up huge farms. People could not own a business or land. They had to work for the government and were poorly paid. The hard-working Vietnamese did not feel they should work long hours for such low wages. Vietnam's economy suffered. Harvests were low, people were unemployed, and the country stayed poor.

New ideas

In 1986, the government realized its plans were not working. It decided to reform its economy by introducing a policy called *doi moi*, which means "new thinking." Some farmers were allowed to rent land, and small family businesses began to appear all over the country.

Trading with the world

In 1989, the Vietnamese government pulled its soldiers from Cambodia. Relations with other countries began to improve. As part of *doi moi*, the government decided to allow foreign companies and banks to set up offices in Vietnam. Countries that had refused to trade with Vietnam now rushed to invest their money in Vietnamese businesses.

(top) Computers are becoming part of some Vietnamese workplaces.
(bottom) Sidewalks and street corners are popular places for hairstylists to set up business. In the past, all businesses were owned by the government.

All kinds of products

Shops, restaurants, and hotels have opened across the country. Small factories manufacture bicycles, glass, bricks, and other products. Artisans create beautiful textiles and ceramics. Street markets are filled with once-scarce fruits and vegetables. Ho Chi Minh City, the center for many new, private businesses, is booming. Young people, wearing the latest fashions, visit the restaurants and karaokes, and the city is full of foreign tourists and business people. Although there are still problems, many people believe that Vietnam will soon become a prosperous nation.

Street stalls, such as this colorful stationery stand, are opening up throughout Vietnamese cities.

Wildlife

Vietnam has a variety of wild animal habitats because it has so many different regions and climates. These habitats are home to over 270 species of mammals, 773 species of birds, and hundreds of species of reptiles and amphibians. Sun bears, monkeys, snakes, tigers, and rhinoceroses live in the lush rain forests. Crocodiles and turtles are found in the tropical swamps of mangrove trees. Sea birds nest in the deltas along the coast, and fish and amphibians thrive in the coral reefs and warm coastal waters.

New, rare, and endangered

New animals are being discovered in Vietnam's remote forests. A rare species of deer, several types of frogs, and a large relative of the cow, called the Vu Quang ox, have been recently identified by scientists. Many of the animals that live in Vietnam's wilderness are endangered, and some species are already extinct. There are no more Sumatran rhinoceroses left in Vietnam, and only about twenty Javan rhinoceroses still survive in the jungle.

Destruction of animal habitats

Vietnam's wilderness is disappearing rapidly. Only a quarter of its ancient forests are left. During the war, many trees were killed by bombing and Agent Orange. Today, loggers are cutting down trees to sell as lumber to other countries, and farmers are clearing forests so they can plant more crops. Trees are also being cut down to be used as firewood for heating and cooking in many homes.

As more tourists visit Vietnam, resorts are being built along the South China Sea. The water is being polluted, and beaches, coral reefs, and mangrove swamps have been destroyed.

Protection

When their homes disappear, animals cannot find food, and they, too, disappear. To protect endangered animal habitats, the government has set aside several national parks where animals are protected. Presently, however, there is not enough money to hire the park staff needed to enforce the conservation laws. The illegal hunting and selling of endangered animals continues.

(opposite page) The douc langur, a rare mammal, is easily recognized by the red-tipped fur on its cheeks.
(right) Some Asian elephants are kept as work animals. Very few survive in Vietnam's wilderness.
(bottom) Sea turtles are illegally hunted, and their shells are used to decorate combs, jewelry, and boxes.

There have been many improvements in Vietnam in the past few years. People are earning more money and are able to buy more of the things they need. Along with improvements, however, there are new challenges.

Pollution

Pollution of the air and water has become a problem in Vietnam, just as it has in other countries. The main reason for pollution is the growing number of businesses in Vietnam. Offices and factories need electricity to make products and operate computers. To get enough electricity, the Vietnamese are building more

energy plants. Unfortunately, many of these plants burn coal to make electricity. Coal creates a black smoke that makes the air very dirty. Motorcycles also add to the pollution problem.

Changing values

As people from Europe and North America visit Vietnam, they introduce their ways of life to the Vietnamese. These new ways are especially attractive to young people. As a result, fashions, music, and attitudes are changing. Some people are afraid that their lives will change so much that their old values will be lost. Others believe that change is a necessary part of progress.

The lives of the Vietnamese are likely to change as they move towards becoming an industrialized nation.

Glossary

altitude The height of the earth's surface above sea level

Buddhism A religion based on the teachings of Buddha, an ancient teacher from India

cash crop A crop grown for sale, to earn money

ceramic Pottery that has been glazed and baked at very high temperatures

Christianity A religion based on the teachings of Jesus Christ

colonial Describing a land or people ruled by another country

colony A land ruled by another country

communism An economic system in which the country's natural resources, businesses, and industry are owned and controlled by the government

corrupt Dishonest

culture The customs, beliefs, and arts of a people

delta An area of land that forms at the mouth of a river due to a build-up of silt, sand, and deposits of rock

dike A wall or bank of earth or rock built to help control flooding

doi moi A term describing Vietnam's new economic ideas and changes

economy The organization and management of a country's businesses, industry, and money

endangered Describing a plant or animal species that could soon become extinct

extinct No longer in existence; no longer living in the wild

habitat The natural environment in which a plant or animal lives

highland A mountainous or hilly area

Indochinese Peninsula The area of land in Southeast Asia that includes Vietnam, Laos, Cambodia, Thailand, Myanmar (Burma), and part of Malaysia

junk A large flat-bottomed sailboat with square sails and a square front

karaoke A form of entertainment in which people sing popular songs to recorded music; a club that features this entertainment

levee A bank of earth or rock, similar to a dike, built to help control flooding

lowland An area that is lower than the land surrounding it

lumber Timber that has been cut into boards and planks

mangrove A type of tropical tree that grows in wet areas such as swamps

manufactured goods Any items that are made in factories using machines

monsoon A system of seasonal winds in Southern Asia

natural resources Materials found in nature, such as oil, coal, minerals, and lumber, which are useful to humans

pagoda A temple that is usually tower-shaped and found in eastern countries. Some pagodas look like several one-story buildings piled on top of one another.

peninsula A point of land that juts into a body of water

plantation A large farm on which only one crop is grown

raw material A substance from the earth that is not yet processed or refined

reform To change something in order to make corrections or improvements

refugee A person who leaves his or her home or country because of danger

sampan A small flat-bottomed boat that has one oar and sometimes one sail at the back

silt A fine sand or clay that is carried and deposited by water

terrace A bank of earth, usually on a hill, with a flat top that is used for growing crops

textile Any type of woven or knitted fabric

torrential Describing a violent flood or stream of water

trade The business of buying, selling, and exchanging goods

Viet Cong South Vietnamese who supported the communist government of the north during the Vietnam War

Index

1 2 3 4 5 6 7 8 9 0 Printed in the USA 5 4 3 2 1 0 9 8 7 6